The Forgotten Deficit

America's Addiction to Foreign Capital

About the International
Economic Policy Association

The International Economic Policy Association, founded in 1957, was the first organization in Washington chartered exclusively to advocate international economic policies of benefit to the nation and American business. It has an ongoing program of researching international balance of payments issues and relating their importance to the well-being of the country. The lack of understanding of the U.S. international payments problem continues to lead to policies which affect the economic strength of our nation and its citizens. In order to shape the debate and build a factual record, the Association carries on a program which analyzes the U.S. balance of payments, U.S. trade and foreign investments, raw materials and international tax problems, and the effects of multinational corporations upon world commerce. IEPA has built its reputation on its expertise in those areas that affect international business and America's position in the world political economy. The Association's support comes entirely from its members who are major U.S.-based multinational corporations. It receives no foreign funding for its reports.

About the Book

The United States is the world's largest debtor nation. An often-overlooked element of the deficit, U.S. capital accounts, is the focus of this critical analysis. The evidence shows that the inflow of foreign money to finance U.S. consumption is going into short- and medium-term, interest-rate-sensitive, liquid instruments. U.S. debt instruments, rather than equities, are the asset of choice.

The authors argue that over the long term this trend will adversely affect the U.S. economy, as every citizen ultimately must constrain consumption to pay the financing charges on the enormous debt buildup. Capital costs in the United States must remain several points higher than in the markets of its major trading competitors. Constraints will be imposed on U.S. policymakers as they attempt to maintain the substantial U.S. economic, political, and military presence overseas.

Divided into an analysis of direct investment and portfolio capital flows, this book contains specific policy recommendations after each section. The authors examine the effect of capital flows on the composition of the U.S. current account transactions with the rest of the world, the linkage of foreign investments to trade, and the effects of protectionism by the Japanese in direct investments.

Published in cooperation with
the International Economic Policy Association

The Forgotten Deficit

America's Addiction to Foreign Capital

Ronald L. Danielian
and Stephen E. Thomsen

Westview Press / Boulder and London

Studies in American Business and the International Economy

This Westview softcover edition is printed on acid-free paper and bound in
softcovers that carry the highest rating of the National Association of
State Textbook Administrators, in consultation with the Association of
American Publishers and the Book Manufacturers' Institute.

Published in 1987 in the United States of America by Westview Press, Inc.;
Frederick A. Praeger, Publisher; 5500 Central Avenue, Boulder, Colorado
80301

Library of Congress Catalog Card Number: 87-50654
ISBN: 0-8133-7450-2

Composition for this book was provided by the authors.
This book was produced without formal editing by the publisher.

Printed and bound in the United States of America

The paper used in this publication meets the requirements
of the American National Standard for Permanence of Paper
for Printed Library Materials Z39.48-1984.

6   5   4   3   2   1

Contents

Tables and Charts

Foreword

Every month headlines display the news, usually bad, about the U.S. trade deficit. Even the man in the street is aware that America faces a long-term structural imbalance in its trading accounts. Capitol Hill buzzes with talk of the need for greater industrial "competitiveness." The Reagan Administration has now conceded that deficits, domestic and foreign, do matter. But outside the professional economic community, there is little talk and even less knowledge about the other major component of the U.S. balance of payments, namely the capital account. This is partly because of its complexity and partly because, as opposed to the flow of goods, financial flows are "invisible." Yet the strategic implications of this other deficit are far-reaching. The fact is that the United States is now the world's largest debtor, financing both a consumption binge and a huge governmental budget deficit with borrowed foreign money. The financing requirements will reduce U.S. GNP, and this becomes at least as serious as the trade problem. Indeed, the two are closely linked.

This paper attempts to de-mystify the subject and its probable future consequences, to analyze the root problems, and to outline potential remedies ranging from greater investment reciprocity to higher domestic savings rates. This study by IEPA's president and economist is part of a special two-year program on "American Business and the International Economy," which has been jointly undertaken by the International Economic Policy Association (IEPA) and the International Economic Studies Institute(IESI). It is designed to correct public misimpressions of America's international economic problems and of the role which the private sector, i.e., American business, can play in developing long-term solutions to those problems. In later reports, attention will be devoted to the industrial production structure needed for national security purposes, as well as for meeting world class competition.

IEPA was founded thirty years ago to foster a coherent foreign economic policy for the United States; IESI was established as an affiliated organization in 1974 to study international economic issues of concern to Americans. Both are non-profit, tax-exempt organizations located in Washington, D.C. As chairman of the former and president of the latter, I want to acknowledge with sincere appreciation the contribution of many corporations, including most of the Association's membership. Thanks also to the General Foods Corporation, IBM, the Ford Motor Company Fund , and foundations, government agencies, and other individuals who have made the program possible. Needless to say, the views in this book are those of the authors and not necessarily those of the people and organizations acknowledged above. But its central theme echoes a concern which is, or should be, felt by all Americans, and indeed the major economic allies of the U.S.

Timothy W. Stanley

Introduction

The United States is the world's largest debtor: U.S. liabilities to foreigners exceed U.S. assets abroad for the first time since 1914. As recently as 1983, the United States had been the world's largest creditor. While these statements merit a good deal of qualification, the important point is that the United States and Japan, with their complementary economic policies, are creating serious imbalances in the international financial system. The problem is not that capital is flowing from a high savings country to a low savings country, for that is as it should be, but rather that international capital is not being put to its best use. Attracted by higher relative interest rates, foreign capital is swarming to the United States to finance the U.S. Government's deficit spending. Foreigners, including the debtor nations, are financing a U.S. consumption boom.

While the United States should not be blamed for any lack of investment opportunities in other countries, we should not continually divert international capital to finance current consumption. We will pay a price for our profligacy in the form of constraints imposed on U.S. policy makers in their attempt to maintain the substantial U.S. economic, political and military presence overseas. The consequences of a continued deficit in our international

accounts are as important as those related to the U.S.
Federal budget deficit. For this reason, securing a better
balance in our current and capital accounts must become one
of our highest priorities.

International capital is created in domestic capital
markets. In order to be a net capital exporter, a nation
must have a surplus in its national savings.[1] If dissavings
exists in an economy, interest rates must rise until national savings equals national investment, or capital must be
imported from overseas. The drain on U.S. savings represented by the Federal budget deficit has reversed the
traditional role of the United States as a capital exporter.
The main supplier of capital to the world and principally to
the United States has been Japan with its unparalleled rate
of savings. Japan's persistent denial of access to its
market for U.S. investment has exacerbated the problem by
denying to the United States a steady stream of investment
income with which to supply the U.S. capital market.

Additionally, capital even has been flowing into the
United States from the developing world in the form of both
capital flight and interest payments. Such a situation is
clearly untenable in the long run.

---

[1]National savings is equal to gross private savings
minus the Government deficit minus gross private domestic
investment.

As a result of the U.S. addiction to foreign capital, policy makers will be constrained by the need to earn foreign exchange and to insure that foreign interest in holding U.S. assets continues. Paul Volcker, Chairman of the Board of Governors of the Federal Reserve System, is most keenly aware of the constraints on monetary policy. In February 1986, he stated before a congressional subcommittee:

> [W]e cannot afford to be complacent. Inevitably, prospects for balance in our internal capital markets -- and therefore prospects for interest rates -- remain for the time being heavily dependent on the willingness of foreigners to place huge amounts of funds in dollars and on the incentives for Americans to employ their money at home. In essence, the financing of both our current account deficit and our internal capital needs -- as long as the government deficit remains so high -- is dependent on a historically high net capital inflow. Clearly, the orderly balancing of our demands for funds with supply in those circumstances requires continued confidence in our currency.[2]

In the long run, the continued reliance on foreign capital to replace that which is swallowed up by the Federal government will place constraints on all branches of Government. The potential problem here is that as the dollar loses some of its status as an international asset, the

---

[2]Statement by Paul A. Volcker, Chairman, Board of Governors of the Federal Reserve System, before the Committee on Banking, Finance and Urban Affairs, U.S. House of Representatives, February 19, 1986.

United States must earn more and more foreign exchange to pay for interest on its foreign debt, for imports and for its continued military presence overseas. Such a scenario is indeed long-term, but it happened to the United Kingdom in the 1960s.[3]

In the short term, should continued budgetary and current account deficits erode confidence in the United States as a place for investment, the United States faces the prospect of higher interest rates. If foreign investors were to withdraw their money in a panic, the United States could face a wrenching recession, causing a further increase in the budget deficit.

Specific recommendations for policy makers are contained in each section. The analysis is divided into two parts comprising the two types of U.S. capital flows: foreign direct investment and portfolio investment. In contrast with an earlier study by the International Economic Policy Association,[4] this report will include the effect of capital flows on the composition of the current account as well as the capital account.

---

[3]See: Albert Imlah, Economic Elements of the Pax Britannica, (Harvard University Press, 1958); Richard Caves et al., Britain's Economic Prospects, (Brookings, 1968).

[4]Stephen E. Thomsen, International Capital Flows and the United States: Palliative, Panacea, or Pandora's Box?, International Economic Policy Association, Washington, D.C., October 1985.

I
Foreign Direct Investment[5]

U.S. foreign direct investment (FDI) is a constant source of foreign exchange for the United States. It also serves as a conduit for one-third of all U.S. merchandise exports, thus providing domestic U.S. employment. U.S. FDI should be recognized as a valuable national asset, but instead it is often criticized or at best ignored. Multilateral and bilateral negotiations have more often centered on trade than on investment. The major exception to this was the 1986 Trade Ministers new GATT round preparatory meeting in Punte del Este. Also, only recently have home and host countries looked seriously at the benefits of direct investment. Finally, the increase in investment in manufacturing by Japanese companies in the United States is bringing to light the need for reciprocity in investment if the United States is ever to restore its current account to health.

From 1948 to 1985, U.S. companies sent $80.5 billion overseas to establish or to acquire operations. Those investments earned $353.0 billion, returning a net $272.5

---

[5]Foreign direct investment is defined as ownership of ten percent of more of the voting stock of a foreign entity. The figures in this section are adjusted for the Netherland Antilles' finance affiliates established to circumvent U.S. withholding taxes that existed until 1984.

billion to the United States in the form of interest, dividends, fees, and royalties (see Table 1).

TABLE 1
Direct Investment Capital Outflow, Income,
and Net Balance, 1948-1985 (millions of dollars)

Year	Net Capital Outflow	Interest, Dividends, Br. Earnings	Fees and Royalties from Affiliated Foreigners	Total Income	Net Balance of Payments Effect
1948 // 1968	33,150	50,627	13,218	63,845	29,695
1969 // 1974	17,687	41,973	12,916	54,889	37,202
1975	6,196	8,547	3,453	12,000	5,804
1976	4,253	11,303	3,531	14,834	10,581
1977	5,612	12,795	3,883	16,678	11,066
1978	4,713	14,115	4,705	18,820	14,107
1979	7,605	19,397	4,980	24,377	16,772
1980	4,915	20,458	5,780	26,238	21,323
1981	-387	20,171	5,794	25,965	26,352
1982	-1,273	18,884	5,561	24,445	25,718
1983	752	15,913	6,275	22,188	21,436
1984	-2,184	17,376	6,530	23,906	26,090
1985	-530	18,028	6,817	24,845	25,375
Totals	80,509	269,587	83,443	353,030	272,521

1. The years 1965-1973 exclude funds borrowed abroad for use by U.S. subsidiaries abroad. Such funds were significant during the period of U.S. direct investment controls (1968-1972).
2. The years 1977-1985 exclude the effects of Netherlands Antilles finance affiliates which are considered as direct investment but actually constitute purchases of foreign securities.
3. Fees and royalties from unaffiliated foreigners are not included in the total. They were $20.3 billion from 1960 to 1985.

Source: U.S. Commerce Department, Survey of Current Business, June issues.

While only $80.5 billion has been sent out of the country since 1948, the U.S. foreign direct investment position (at book value) has increased by almost $225 billion during that time. The difference is made up by reinvested earnings.

The U.S. investment position stood at $252.5 billion in 1985, compared with foreign investment in the United States worth $175.8 billion.[6] In 1985, our investments overseas returned $25.4 billion over and above direct investment outflows. Investment by foreign companies in the United States also provided a net inflow of capital of $7.4 billion in 1985. For the time being, heavy Japanese investment in 1985, primarily in automobile production has dwarfed the outflows resulting from repatriated profits by foreigners.

Eventually, even though they may be contributing to employment and growth here, as these subsidiaries of foreign companies in the United States mature, they are going to represent a net drain on our balance of payments. This is particularly true in the case of Japan, where U.S. companies are often effectively blocked from investing. The result will be a continued erosion of our current account balance with that country even as our bilateral trade balance improves. The facts show that while foreign investment in the U.S. economy is beneficial, investment

------

[6]Foreign direct investment is recorded at book value. As U.S. foreign direct investment is generally older than foreign direct investment here, the figures are not completely comparable. Judged at market value, the U.S. overall investment position would probably look much better.

reciprocity is vital to our future balance of payments. The issue of reciprocity will taken up at the end of this section.

U.S. Direct Investment in Developing Countries

Just as investment by foreigners in the United States benefits our economy, excepting the possible balance of payments concerns stemming from the absence of reciprocity, U.S. FDI overseas benefits the host country's economy. Nevertheless, foreign direct investment, principally by U.S. multinational corporations (MNCs), has long been a subject of controversy. U.S. MNCs have been criticized at various times by governments of both industrial and developing countries, as well as by groups within the home country, notably labor unions. To formulate recommendations for U.S. policies toward direct investment by and in the United States, it is necessary to show not only the advantages of such investment to both the home and host countries, but also to disprove many of the emotional arguments against MNC investment in foreign countries.

Investment by U.S. MNCs in developing countries (LDCs), though only 23 percent of total U.S. foreign direct investment, receives the most international attention. In general, MNCs bring capital, technology, expertise and employment to LDCs. By purchasing goods and services locally and by paying above average wages, MNCs also serve to stimulate growth in those countries in which they invest. To the extent that MNCs export what they produce they improve the trade performance of the host country. They are, in effect, a ready-made, efficient industry for a country that would have difficulty creating one on its own.

Critics of MNCs claim that foreign affiliates of MNCs do not belong to the country in which they are located; they are allegedly "pirates without flag or country," with little regard for the host country beyond its profit-making potential. This argument was especially pervasive during the 1970s. MNCs must bear some of the burden for this misconception fostered by a few well-publicized cases of MNC involvement in influencing domestic politics of developing countries. Critics also contend that MNCs may actually hinder economic development by draining the host country of capital, by orienting the economy towards the production of luxury goods, and by employing only outmoded or "inappropriate" technology. Yet, if we are to assume that foreign investment in LDCs is a long-term prospect for an MNC, then a continuous injection of new capital and technology is a necessity.

While the MNC-LDC debate continues, relations between the two have evolved since the hostility of the 1970s. It is no longer surprising to see LDCs publicizing foreign investment opportunities in their countries in U.S. business periodicals. Mexico, for example, placed a six-page advertisement in the Wall Street Journal on June 23, 1986, listing Mexican investment possibilities. The change of heart has come about primarily as a result of the debt crisis. These countries have learned the

obvious advantage of equity over debt when foreign capital is
needed: while debt implies fixed payments, equity dividends are
tied to performance. Ironically, the same debts which have fueled
the increased interest of LDCs in foreign investment have also
discouraged MNCs from investing there. The imposed austerity
measures breed uncertainty and instability, and the developing
countries' need for foreign exchange leads to restrictions on both
the repatriation of investment earnings and the importation of
needed capital goods.

These restrictions, along with other performance requirements, clearly are not in the interests of the United States and,
as they serve to discourage foreign investment, are counter-
productive for the host country. Other restrictions include
export requirements, local content and employment, and technology
transfer. Table 2 shows the prevalence of requirements in several
major developing countries.

TABLE 2

Performance Requirements and Investments
in Developing Countries

U.S. Foreign Investment-Manufacturing			Requirements (% of nonbank affiliates of U.S. nonbank parents affected in 1982)					
Country	Growth 79-84 (percent)	Position 1984 ($millions)	(1)	(2)	(3)	(4)	(5)	(6)
Singapore	245	1013	1	0	0	2	3	0
Malaysia	239	370	6	1	4	33	11	0
Hong Kong	112	629	0	0	0	0	2	0
Taiwan	84	464	10	0	2	5	8	3
Panama	61	344	1	0	1	13	2	1
Ecuador	56	142	0	1	1	17	8	3
Indonesia	48	152	2	2	3	23	38	2
Colombia	46	719	6	0	1	19	8	3
Argentina	43	1695	1	1	2	5	6	1
Brazil	34	6544	1	19	4	32	6	11
Mexico	16	3988	5	5	4	14	8	9
S. Korea	-3	211	7	1	7	13	13	4
Philippines	-11	443	6	3	3	3	6	3
Venezuela	-23	722	1	2	4	41	9	2

Requirements:
1. Export minimum
2. Import limit
3. Local content
4. Local employment
5. Technology transfer
6. Ratio of exchange earnings to exchange expenditures

Sources: U.S. Commerce Department: Survey of Current Business, August issues; U.S. Direct Investment Abroad: 1982 Benchmark Survey Data, Dec. 1985.

By distorting trade and investment flows, such policies are inimical to global economic interests. The United States should work multilaterally through GATT and bilaterally through bilateral investment treaties (BITs) to remove such distortions. We have lagged behind Europe in negotiating BITs with Third World countries, but the gap is narrowing as we now have ten treaties signed and several more in the works, all with developing countries. The U.S. Senate is expected to ratify several of them this year. Unfortunately, no BITs have been signed with the major countries of Latin America. Together, Brazil and Mexico account for 11 percent of U.S. foreign direct investment in manufacturing.

The objective of the BITs is to provide for inter-governmental consultation on problems, arbitration of investment disputes, national treatment (non-discrimination against the foreign firm in the local market), reasonable assurances about repatriation of capital and profits, and adequate compensation in the event of nationalization or expropriation; but negotiations have been arduous. With China, for example, there are still issues to be resolved even after six rounds of talks. Appendix I contains an example of a bilateral investment treaty.

One unfortunate omission from the bilateral treaties is a clause concerning reciprocity. Without such a reciprocity clause, asymmetric investment patterns with such countries as Japan will be amplified. Nevertheless, by removing some of the more blatant investment requirements of our trading partners, the BITs will serve some purpose.

In addition to curbing these performance requirements, the United States also should push for greater U.S. foreign investment in these countries as a way of supplying foreign capital without adding to debt obligations. For this reason, the United States should promote the Multilateral Investment Guarantee Agency (MIGA) of the World Bank. The MIGA will guarantee against four types of risk: restrictions on the amount an MNC affiliate can transfer back home, expropriation, breach of contract by the host country, and war or civil unrest. MIGA also will publicize investment opportunities and offer technical assistance to developing countries. To avoid giving an unfair advantage to MNCs over the local competition, MIGA also will cover funds brought into the country by local competitors. Action is needed by five developed and 15 developing countries, subscribing a total of $360 million. Owing to the need for Congress to appropriate $44 million of the $222 million U.S. subscription, there is some question whether the almost necessary U.S. blessing will be forthcoming in spite of Administration support. The House Banking Committee of the U.S. Congress has decided to put off the Administration's request for funding for MIGA until next year, mainly due to budgetary restraints. MIGA is intended as a complement to the International Centre for Settlement of Investment Disputes (ICSID). Both serve to promote investment: MIGA by providing guarantees and the ICSID by providing an international forum for dispute settlement.

Although U.S. MNCs can generally protect themselves against many commercial and political risks through the U.S. Overseas Private Investment Corporation (OPIC), as can many European firms through their governments' analogous programs, the coverage is not complete. Moreover, it is argued, host countries are more comfortable with a multilateral program. Reagan administration efforts to "privatize" OPIC will increase the need for MIGA. Currently, OPIC is cheaper and offers better coverage than private insurers. If it is privatized, it will probably lose some of its negotiating power in settlement disputes.

Finally, to promote investment over debt as a source of foreign capital and to expand U.S. exports to Latin America, the U.S. Government should push for a more equal sharing of Latin American payments. Rather than devoting precious foreign exchange solely to interest payments, part should be given to subsidiaries of U.S. firms to pay dividends to the parent company and part should be used by the debtor nation to purchase imports. Such an approach would be consistent with the philosophy of Chapter 11 bankruptcy proceedings which recognizes that creditors often strive for short-term gains, usually liquidation of the debtor's assets, at the expense of a greater stream of income in the future.

The Argument that U.S. Foreign Investment Exports Jobs

Unions have argued that foreign direct investment harms the home country of the parent by "exporting jobs" in order to take advantage of cheaper foreign labor and by exporting manufactured goods back to the home market, especially in the United States. According to the AFL-CIO, the consequences of such actions are grim:

> The great exodus of American production to overseas plants has led economists, labor leaders, and even some farsighted businessmen to wonder whether we are witnessing the dimming of America. This greatest industrial power in the world's history is in danger of becoming nothing more than a nation of hamburger stands...a country stripped of industrial capacity and meaningful work...a service economy...a nation of citizens busily buying and selling cheeseburgers and root beer floats.[7]

Studies have refuted this claim by showing that companies with foreign investments have actually created more jobs at home than those with no international investment, owing to the fact that at least one-third of U.S. exports

---

[7]"U.S. Multinationals—The Dimming of America," a report by the AFL-CIO submitted at hearings before the Subcommittee on International Trade of the U.S. Senate Finance Committee, February, 1973, p. 448.

are to foreign affiliates.[8] Also, the latest available Commerce Department Benchmark Survey (1982) found that only 9.7 percent of goods produced by manufacturing affiliates are exported back to the United States. When transportation equipment from Canadian affiliates (under the U.S.-Canadian Automotive Agreement) is excluded, the figure is closer to five percent. As the overvalued dollar forces companies to "outsource," increasingly to overseas locations, in order to compete with imports from countries with undervalued currencies, this relatively small figure can be expected to increase in later data.

Generally speaking, MNCs would prefer to service foreign markets from a U.S. production base if that is feasible. But increasingly, when faced with impediments such as the common tariff barrier of the European Community or the elaborate systems of exchange and other controls of Latin America, or distance and shipping costs putting them at a competitive disadvantage, companies have tended to produce abroad for those markets and, often urged by the

---

[8]See: Robert Hawkins, Job Displacement and the Multinational Firm: A Methodological Review, Center for Multinational Studies, Occasional Paper No. 3, June 1972; or The Effects of U.S. Corporate Foreign Investment 1971-79, Business International, July 1981.

host country's desire to earn foreign exchange, to export to third countries.[9]

Foreign Direct Investment Among Industrial Nations

The issue of foreign direct investment among industrial countries is vastly different from that concerning investment in developing countries. The important distinction is that the major industrial countries all have MNCs with substantial investments in each others' economies (see Table 3), thus reciprocity is a vital issue. While few doubt the political power of the governments in the industrial countries to control foreign investment within their borders, such investment can at times elicit either fears of economic hegemony or xenophobia, such as with the U.S. reaction to Arab purchases of U.S. real estate in the 1970s. In 1967, the Frenchman Jean-Jacques Servan-Schreiber wrote Le Defi Americain (The American Challenge) in response to the tremendous increase in U.S. foreign investment in Europe following the formation of the European Community (EC) in 1957. The threat was thought to be one of superior

---

[9]For a more complete analysis of this subject, see: Timothy W. Stanley and Stephen E. Thomsen, "Evaluating the MNC Contribution, The Harvard International Review, April 1986.

managerial prowess and greater technological ability on the part of American business. He claimed, "We see a foreign challenger breaking down the political and psychological framework of our societies. We are witnessing the prelude to our own historical bankruptcy."[10] To counter such a threat, he suggested selectively imitating the flexibility of the American economy.

---

[10]Jean-Jacques Servan-Schreiber, The American Challenge, trans. by Ronald Steel (London: Hamish Hamilton, 1967), p. xiii.

TABLE 3

U.S. Direct Investment Position, Selected Countries, 1985
(book value; millions of dollars)

Country	U.S. Direct Investment Position Abroad	Foreign Direct Investment in the United States
Canada	46,435	16,678
France	7,835	6,295
Germany	16,746	14,417
Italy	5,644	1,401
Netherlands	7,064	36,124
U.K.	33,963	43,766
Switzerland	16,230	11,040
Japan	9,095	19,116
Developed	172,750	164,296
Developing	54,474	18,655
Total	227,224	182,951

Source: U.S. Commerce Department, Survey of Current Business, August issues.

Another more recent U.S. example might be termed "Le Defi Japonais." Japanese automobile producers are now important producers in the United States. Just as with the fears of Servan-Schreiber, some are suggesting that we try to follow the Japanese example, either by establishing a U.S. MITI (Ministry of International Trade and Investment) or by adopting Japanese management techniques.

While the sensationalist fears of "Le Defi Japonais" are as unfounded as "Le Defi Americain" was in 1967, the skewed nature of investment flows between Japan and the United States is every bit as important as the well publicized bilateral trade deficit. In fact, the more concealed

and long term nature of the investment imbalance may make it
the more pernicious of the two. Since the Japanese use
foreign investments as a channel for their exports much more
than do U.S. companies, the lack of reciprocity in investment flows aggravates the trade problem.

Based on 1984 figures in Table 4, while U.S. affiliates
in Japan imported $2.9 billion from the United States,
Japanese affiliates in the United States imported $47.3
billion from Japan. In other words, 79 percent of all Japanese exports to the United States were to their U.S. affiliates and only 12.4 percent of U.S. exports were to American
affiliates in Japan. That is less that half of the overall
U.S. average.

Typically, the Japanese restrict foreign investment in
nascent industries. Despite repeated attempts by U.S.
automobile companies to invest in Japan in the 1960s, they
were allowed to enter only after the Japanese had developed
a mature and competitive automobile industry based on world
demand and not domestic markets.

Table 4

THE EFFECT OF NONRECIPROCITY IN INVESTMENT:
JAPAN AND THE UNITED STATES
1984
($ millions)

	Investment Position (Book Value) (1)	U.S. Exports Shipped to all U.S. Affiliates in Japan (2)	of which to majority-owned affiliates (3)	Japanese Exports Shipped to all Japanese Affiliates in the U.S. (4)	Japanese Total Exports to US (5)	U.S. Total Exports to Japan (6)	Percent of Trade Due to Investments %
American Investments in Japan	7,920	2,890	(2,231)			23,241	12.4% (col.2 - 6) 9.6%* (col.3 - 6)
Japanese investments in the U.S.	16,044			47,275	60,210		79% (col.4 - 5)

*Most Japanese investments in the U.S. are through majority ownership such as in auto manufacturing. Thus, this 9.6 percent figure is valid as a comparison against the Japanese 79 percent figure.

SOURCE: U. S. Department of Commerce, Survey of Current Business, various issues.

The same pattern can be seen more recently in telecommunications, satellites, biotechnology and securities trading. In fact, Japanese banks and security houses were afforded near complete access to the United States market some three to four years before U.S. businesses were given partial access to their market. Furthermore, Japan still employs an elaborate investment approval process, permits only joint ventures except in very limited circumstances and prevents foreign ownership of more than 50 percent in its energy companies or more than 25 percent in its technologically innovative companies.[11]

The Japanese exhibit the same ethnocentricity and sense of national purpose with their investments in other countries. They tend to keep the foreign exchange earnings within the same family. A Japanese automobile producer, for example, will establish operations in the United States, initially importing almost everything. According to Assistant Secretary of Commerce H. P. Goldfield, 80 percent of the parts in Japanese cars produced in the United States are imported.[12] Almost another 10 percent is provided by their own captive suppliers.

---

[11] John Bryant, Member, U.S. Congress, News Conference Statement on "The Foreign Investment Disclosure and Reciprocity Act," May 30, 1985.

[12] Washington Post, May 8, 1986.

U.S. imports of motor vehicle parts and accessories from Japan mushroomed from $1.8 billion in 1981 to $4.2 billion in 1985 (including $1.2 billion in foreign trade zone imports by Japanese manufacturers). Ultimately, the parts are supplied by new Japanese investors set up around the primary company, possibly supplanting local suppliers.

Many of these new Japanese suppliers are owned by the automobile companies themselves. Thus, the establishment in the United States of such companies as Stanley Electric, Bellemar, Nihon Radiator, Calsonic, and other companies to provide air conditioners, radiators, headlights, taillights, seats and mufflers is part of the pattern. All of these companies are majority-owned Japanese firms or "captive" suppliers, and their presence here will affect our international accounts and future American domestic business. For instance, at present, although there is excess U.S. glass-making capacity, yet U.S. located Japanese automobile company's incremental production needs will be supplied by a new Japanese-owned glass company. Currently, an American company, PPG Industries, is the sole U.S. supplier of glass for the automobile company. From now on, however, PPG Industries will have only a 20 percent interest in supplying any future production of auto glass as a minority partner.

The Need for Reciprocity in Investment

As mentioned earlier, foreign direct investment is a vital component of trade flows, serving as a conduit for exports. Therefore, any persistent imbalance in investment flows amplifies the lopsidedness in trade flows. What is needed is a balance in both trade and direct investment between the United States and other countries. Our goods, services, and investments should enjoy the same opportunities in other countries that their foreign counterparts enjoy here, namely a relatively open market and few investment restrictions. But such has not been the case, and nowhere is the discrepancy more pronounced than with Japan.

The resistance of the Japanese to allowing U.S. investments may have been a contributing factor to the skewed nature of our bilateral trade. In the 1960s, U.S. auto companies tried in vain to invest in Japan. If U.S. companies had been free to invest then, our automobile trade picture would look much different today in terms of the enormous drain on the U.S. international accounts. At a minimum, a portion of the income earned from imports of Japanese cars would have accrued to the United States, to U.S. automobile companies, and their workers. In Europe, if U.S. companies were unable to export, they could make the sale by investing and producing locally. The same complementary relationship between trade and investment in open markets was never given a chance to develop with Japan.

Table 5 shows U.S. exports to majority-owned foreign affiliates (MOFAs) abroad and the total foreign sales of U.S. MOFAs. This table compares Japanese investment statistics for 1982 with those of France and Germany, whose combined GDP and population are roughly equal to Japan's. All other Pacific rim nations, excluding Australia and New Zealand, are included as a reference. Based on the size and maturity of the economies, there is a decided imbalance in the foreign investment operations among the areas compared. For an economy as large and wealthy as that of Japan, the figures contained in the table belie any claim that Japan is truly open. Preliminary figures for 1984 show the same disparities.

In comparison with our relationships with other nations, the U.S.-Japanese relationship is in trouble. Our trade has been in deficit and we have been unable to make up the difference by investment. We are moving into an era when the United States will face heavy trade and very large investment deficits wherein our current account will remain in deficit. To avoid trade protectionism, Japan has stepped up its direct investment here, a move which coincidentally is politically strategic. In automobiles and accessory parts, for instance, plants have been built or are planned for in seven states representing 14 U.S. senators and affecting almost one third of all congressional districts. Yet without reciprocal access to the Japanese market for U.S. companies, their investments here can exacerbate the trade deficit.

26

Table 5

U.S. MAJORITY-OWNED FOREIGN AFFILIATES COMPARISON, SALES, INVESTMENT AND REPATRIATED INCOME
1982

($ millions)

	U.S. MNC Exports Shipped to Affiliates	Total MNC Sales by Foreign Affiliates	U.S. Overall Merchandise Trade Balance	U.S. Direct Investment Position	U.S. Direct Investment Repatriated Income
Japan	1,527	25,788	-16,989	3,360	+370
GDP Surrogate[1]	4,937	108,652	-1,026	20,858	+1,454
France	2,203	41,404	+1,663	6,860	+416
W. Germany	2,734	67,248	-2,689	13,998	+1,038
Asia & Pacific [excl. Australia, New Zealand and Japan]	4,494	48,903	-5,293	9,663	+2,445

Note: 1982 is used as a reference date because 1983 detailed figures for France and Germany were unavailable. Based on past years, however, it is unlikely that there would be a major change in the disparities.

[1] France and West Germany together equal the approximate population size and gross domestic product of Japan.

SOURCE: Survey of Current Business, U.S. Department of Commerce, various issues.

What is needed to correct this imbalance is reciprocity; used 53 years ago to expand markets.

In 1934, the Reciprocal Trade Agreements Program was based on the Trade Agreements Act (June 12, 1934) which empowered the President to enter into trade agreements through reciprocal adjustment of trade barriers. After the Great Depression, and in reaction to the protectionist Smoot-Hawley Act, the general objective of the trade agreements program was to substitute economic cooperation for economic warfare in our relations with foreign nations.

The idea of negotiations with other countries for the reduction of excessive barriers to foreign trade was considered more practical than the immediate revision of U.S. tariff laws alone. To follow up on the trade agreements program and have the fullest involvement of interested persons (including U.S. businesses), Executive Order 6750, issued June 27, 1934, under Section 4 of the Trade Agreements Act, established the Committee for Reciprocity Information. The issue of reciprocity in the trade area, including the trade definitions of reciprocal concessions or reciprocal trade, has been understood since 1934 to mean the exchange of roughly equal or equivalent concessions between countries.

According to Philip Trezise of the Brookings Institution, "Reciprocity need only mean balanced opportunities to trade. That indeed is a sensible objective. The GATT rests squarely on the principle of reciprocal bargains."[13] Without reciprocity in both trade and investment, protectionist sentiment and economic dislocations will build, thus forcing the possibility of political reactions with worse economic consequences. In effect, reciprocity is simply the process of opening up markets.

The U.S. Government should develop a new investment policy to work more aggressively toward an open world economy by calling for stricter reciprocity and by selectively providing mechanisms to convince other countries to give greater national treatment in their own economies. The ground rules should be stated up front with an open-door policy as the objective and with a rebuttable presumption that a foreign nation currently affords U.S. companies nondiscriminatory, reciprocal treatment. If it is shown that there is a persistent denial of reciprocity and of national treatment, then there should be a policy review mechanism that could affect that country's investments in the United States. But, any arbitrary measures taken by the United States against foreign investment here would have to be evaluated very carefully to make sure that the net effect is not adverse to our economy.

_____

[13] Philip Trezise, editorial in The Washington Post, February 11, 1982.

There is presently an interagency committee that reviews foreign investment matters called the Committee on Foreign Investments in the United States (CFIUS), established in 1976 by President Ford. The CFIUS should continue to collect information and to review investment problems with the necessary legal authority to require information on inward flows. No new bureaucracy should be created, except for a centralized industry liaison office where American business can bring forward complaints and offer information in cases where they believe their investments overseas are not being treated in accordance with the standards for foreign investment in the United States. Service industries should be included as they are a significant and growing portion of U.S. international commerce.

Foreign investment here also should meet all applicable FTC (Federal Trade Commission) and SEC (Securities and Exchange Commission) regulations. A factual accounting for statistical purposes, such as under the International Investment Survey Act, would greatly benefit the general understanding among legislators of the significance of foreign direct investment.

To guide overall policy there needs to be more effective and centralized coordination at the White House level, such as a revived Council on International Economic Policy, chaired by the U.S. Trade Representative in his capacity as the senior presidential advisor on international trade and investment. Reorganization Plan No. 3 of 1979, redesignating the Special Representative for Trade Negotiations as the United States Trade Representative, vested in him the authority "for developing and for coordinating the implementation of U.S. international trade policy, including commodity matters and, to the extent they are related to international trade policy, direct investment matters."

Considering the foreign policy ramifications of U.S. actions on foreign investment, it is obvious that the State Department will have to be closely involved as will the Departments of Commerce and Treasury. However, one individual, the USTR, must be responsible for taking the overall policy lead.

For foreign investments in the United States with national security considerations, because of the growing number of government-owned or -controlled corporations engaging in international trade and investment, additional U.S. Government monitoring is necessary. The 1982 Kuwaiti purchase of Santa Fe International would be included in this category as Santa Fe's Braun subsidiary was involved in sensitive nuclear research. These investments also would be subject to the previously-outlined reciprocity review and to all applicable U.S. regulations. Chart 1 (at the end of this report) analyzes in a matrix form the four major categories of foreign investment in the United States.

As explained in Chart 1, direct investment in the United States by government-controlled companies in sensitive areas such as telecommunications, aviation, defense, and energy resources should require formal notification and review. For foreign government investment in nonsensitive areas, a requirement for prenotification to CFIUS is all that would be necessary. This prenotification is necessary because government-controlled corporations may not operate on a purely commercial, profit-oriented basis. Their operations (such as in pricing and marketing) may be guided by non-business objectives.

CHART 1

MATRIX OF FOREIGN INVESTMENT IN THE U.S.

Investor \ Sector	Sensitive	Non-sensitive
Government-owned or controlled corporation	Formal notification and review by present U.S. government structure. Approval needed for investment to be consummated. CFIUS and USTR to be lead group.	Pre-notification only. No formal approval needed. However, reciprocity objection could be lodged by U.S. industry or USTR which, if the facts and circumstances warrant, could lead to holding up the investment. Objective same as below.
Foreign-owned private investor	Notification and review with presumption that investment can be made. No formal approval needed but within 60 days, objection could be raised by present U.S. government structure.	Notification for statistical data purposes only, no formal review. Possibility of U.S. private companies or USTR entering a reciprocity objection before present U.S. agencies. Objective of free flow of investment should be primary goal.

II
Portfolio Capital[14]

The international economic events of the last five years are intricately linked with the rapid growth of capital mobility. Although there is no reliable way of knowing, gross international capital movements are estimated to surpass $20 trillion annually. They have grown exponentially since the advent of floating exchange rates in 1973 and the gradual liberalization of the world's major capital markets in Europe, Japan, and the United States. Capital movements may force greater macroeconomic coordination among the industrial nations which will prove beneficial in the long run. In the short run, however, the lack of harmony in the economic policies of Europe, Japan and the United States has destabilized the global economy and must, therefore, be addressed.

---

[14]Portfolio capital is comprised mostly of banking flows and securities transactions. The degree of liquidity varies with each financial instrument, but many have highly developed secondary markets, the one exception being debt of developing countries.

The Growth in International Capital Mobility

The growth in capital flows has been spurred on by financial deregulation, innovation, and technological advances. The United States has been the cynosure of these changes over the last decade, compelling and inviting other countries to imitate U.S. initiatives. Following the end of fixed exchange rates in 1973, the Nixon administration abandoned the credit controls that had been promulgated in the 1960s in the vain hope of improving the U.S. balance of payments. From 1963 to 1974, an interest equalization tax (IET) discouraged purchases of foreign securities by U.S. residents by imposing, initially, a 15 percent tax on the actual value of stocks at the time of the transfer and a tax of up to 15 percent on bond issues depending on the maturity. The IET negated the advantages for foreigners of offering securities in the United States because of the low U.S. interest rates relative to the other major countries.

In addition, from 1965 to 1968 there was a "voluntary" restraint on U.S. foreign direct investment. From 1968 to 1974, the restraint was mandatory. Large commercial banks were also prevented from lending more than 103 percent of their foreign credit outstanding at year-end 1964. President Nixon's reasons (as stated in 1968) for ending the restraints and the IET were as follows:

> While I in no way want to minimize the gravity of the balance of payments crisis, I feel that the

imposition of arbitrary controls on foreign investments is harmful to our nation's long range interests. This control program is a palliative, which may make the statistics look better now, but will only further aggravate our balance of payments in future years.[15]

The removal of these controls was only the first step in the gradual process of deregulation. In 1975, the United States ended fixed commissions on stock transactions, allowing firms to both broker and sell on their own account. Other domestic deregulation that was to have international consequences occurred in the banking sector, where Regulation Q, which placed a ceiling of 5.25 percent on interest paid to depositors, was repealed in 1980. Previously, banks had always been provided with an almost free source of capital. In fact, in the highly inflationary 1970s, banks were paying a negative real rate of interest on certain deposits.

In the last few years, the legislative walls between commercial and investment banks, savings and loan institutions, stockbrokerage firms, and insurance companies have begun to crumble. Financial institutions have found ways to circumvent such antiquated legislation as the Glass-Steagall Act preserving the distinction between commercial and investment banks, and the McFadden Act prohibiting commercial banks from engaging in interstate banking.

---

[15]Letter from Richard Nixon to N.R. Danielian, October 3, 1968.

Another change in U.S. regulations occurred in 1978 when pension fund managers were allowed to invest overseas. Such institutional investors are responsible for three-quarters of all stock purchases in the United States. Their desire to diversify their portfolios internationally has spawned greater capital mobility. As a result, more and more foreign firms (particularly British, Dutch and Japanese, but now also French) are listed on the New York Stock Exchange where one-half of the global equity market is located.

The greatest step taken by the Reagan administration in the direction of deregulation was the 1984 repeal of the U.S. withholding tax on interest paid to foreigners, probably motivated by the U.S. Treasury's exceptional financing needs. As a result, France, Germany, and Japan all eliminated their withholding taxes the same year. Although the effect of the repeal was mitigated by the fact that some capital previously had circumvented the tax, the repeal was doubtless an important stimulus for foreign purchases of U.S. Treasury and corporate securities. The tax had formerly constituted an increased cost of borrowing abroad for a local resident.

The financial centers in other industrial nations have all slowly followed the U.S. example. By the end of the 1970s, the United Kingdom, Canada, Switzerland, and Germany all had removed their controls on capital. In October 1986, ten years after the United States, the United Kingdom ended

fixed commissions on stock transactions. In March 1986, the
United Kingdom allowed foreign firms to become full members
on the London Stock Exchange. In Tokyo, only a few U.S.
stock brokerage firms finally have been accorded the
opportunity to bid for seats on the Tokyo exchange, a privilege that foreign firms in New York have enjoyed for four
years.

Japan has been one of the most reluctant deregulators,
preferring capital controls which in turn affect currency
values. Foreigners were permitted to purchase certain
Japanese securities only after the rapid depreciation of the
yen in 1979. In 1984, at the behest of the U.S. Treasury,
the Japanese began a new policy of liberalizing the restrictions on both inflows and outflows of capital.[16] These
measures included a relaxation of rules governing the
issuance of yen-denominated Samurai bonds by foreigners
wishing to borrow in Japan. In June 1986, Citicorp became
the first foreign bank to float Euroyen bonds following a
new Japanese policy that permits such flotations providing
that the proceeds are not brought into Japan (which would
increase the value of the yen). Most Japanese banks are
still not permitted to issue Euroyen bonds.

---

[16] While capital flows were deregulated, the domestic
interest rate structure in Japan was still closely
controlled by government policy. Thus, a currency outflow
or inflow did not always have the requisite effect on the
exchange rate.

Japan also eliminated the limit on yen lending overseas by Japanese banks and eased certain restrictions on foreign direct investment and real estate investment in Japan. Beginning in 1986, Japanese pension funds are now permitted to invest 25 percent of their funds in foreign assets, up from 10 percent. Another request of the U.S. Treasury was for an internationalization of the yen in order to push up the demand for the yen and cause it to appreciate, assuming the supply of yen does not rise enough to offset the increased demand. An internationalization of the yen is not without risks for the United States. These risks will be discussed later.

Given the strong divergence in national savings rates between the United States and Japan, deregulation in Japan has greatly increased the demand for U.S. dollar assets in the short run.

Finally, in the European capital market, the President of the European Community Commission, Jacques Delors, has called for gradual progress towards a unified capital market within the EC. Some major EC countries already have fairly open capital markets, but the proposal will meet with resistance from such countries as Ireland, Spain, Greece, Portugal and Italy.

In all the major capital markets, innovation has been stimulated by the increased competition that deregulation leaves in its wake. Much of this innovation has been motivated by the desire of investors to minimize risk. Included are floating rate notes (which convert interest risk into credit risk), currency and interest rate swaps, financial futures contracts, forward-market operations, options, trading in entitlements, insurance of credit risk, etc. By serving to minimize potential risk to the investor, these innovations have fostered foreign investment.

International Banking Flows

The initial surge in international capital stemmed from excess U.S. dollar liabilities abroad (fueled by U.S. deposits) and the creation of the Eurodollar market, both in the 1960s. Beginning in the 1970s, banks were faced with declining opportunities and increased competition at home, a need to provide more services to their major clients (the increasingly financially independent multinational corporations), and finally a need to recycle billions of petro-dollars through the maturing Eurodollar market. These forces, when combined with the ubiquitous "herd instinct" that is better explained by sociologists than by economists, led to the tremendous growth in international banking in the last decade.

While U.S. bank liabilities to foreigners have remained fairly constant over time, U.S. bank claims, principally loans, have dropped from $111 billion in 1982 to $0.7

billion in 1985.[17] Loans by banks in the United States to debtor countries in the developing world have virtually stopped (see Table 6). Furthermore, given the problems with bank soundness and the improved sophistication of corporate financial managers, many U.S. corporations have turned to the bond market for funding.

---

[17]Some have concluded from this fact that the tremendous capital inflows are not foreign capital but instead returning U.S. assets attracted by the bright growth prospects in the United States. In fact, the largest component of capital inflows in 1984 and 1985 was foreign purchases of U.S. securities. Net securities inflows exceeded net banking flows by $11 billion in 1984 and $24 billion in 1985.

TABLE 6

Foreign Claims and Liabilities Reported by Banks
in the United States[18]
(millions of dollars)

	Claims	Liabilities
1985	691	40,387
1984	8,504	31,674
1983	29,928	49,341
1982	111,070	65,922
1981	84,175	42,128
1980	46,838	10,743
1979	26,213	32,607
1978	33,667	16,141

Source: U.S. Commerce Department, Survey of
Current Business.

---

[18] Banks in the United States are not all U.S.-owned.
The distinction is not important for balance of payments
purposes, but it is interesting to note that while U.S.-
owned banks in the United States reduced their own claims on
foreigners by $7.7 billion in 1985, foreign banks in the
United States increased their own claims on non-U.S. residents by $10.5 billion. Therefore, at the moment, foreign
banks in the United States are contributing more to our
long-term balance of payments than our own banks.

In an effort to recapture their clients, banks have
begun to offer a more global line of services such as
international financial consulting, and worldwide credit
checks and clearinghouse services. Banks also have begun to
promote Euronotes, which are short-term negotiable
money-market notes resembling commercial paper and offering
funds at a rate close to that at which banks lend to each
other. So far $11 billion of such notes have been issued.

International Securities Transactions

International banking flows reflect the retrenchment by
banks in the United States. As Table 7 indicates, international syndicated loans have dropped from $98.2 billion in
1982 to $42.0 billion in 1985. In contrast, international
bond issues increased from $75.5 billion in 1982 to $167.7
billion in 1985. International bond offerings are continuing at an annual rate of $200 billion in 1986.

TABLE 7

International Capital Market Indicators
(billion of dollars)

	1982	1983	1984	1985
Floating-rate bond issues	15.3	19.5	38.2	58.4
Other bond offerings	60.2	57.6	73.3	109.3
Syndicated loans	98.2	67.2	57.0	42.0
Note issuance and other back-up facilities	5.4	9.5	28.8	46.8
Total Borrowing	179.1	153.8	197.3	256.5

Source: OECD, Financial Market Trends.

The United States is the largest player in the international bond market, owing to the size of the U.S. economy and to the net deficit in domestic U.S. savings. In the public sector, as Table 8 indicates, foreigners have purchased over $50 billion of U.S. Treasury securities since the beginning of 1984. The Japanese have accounted for over half of this amount, buying $19 billion of securities from the U.S. Treasury in 1985 compared with $6.1 billion in 1984. Preliminary figures for the first quarter of 1986 show net Japanese purchases of long-term U.S. Treasury securities equaling only $0.9 billion, resulting from the strong appreciation of the yen during that period and from the declining interest rate differential. Nevertheless, foreign purchases of U.S. Treasury securities are running at a record annual rate of $33.2 billion (based on first quarter figures).

TABLE 8

Net Foreign Purchases of U.S. Treasury Securities
(billions of dollars)

	Private Purchases	Official Purchases
1986 (first quarter)	(8.3)	(3.1)*
1985	20.5	-0.6
1984	22.4	4.7
1983	8.7	7.0
1982	7.1	5.8
1981	2.9	5.0
1980	2.6	9.7
1979	5.0	-22.4
1978	2.2	23.6

*Includes all Government securities.

Source: U.S. Commerce Department, Survey of Current Business.

Japan's continued, albeit substantially diminished, interest in U.S. Treasury securities, even after a 35 percent depreciation of the yen against the dollar, can be attributed to a number of factors. First, Japan is eager to minimize the political friction with the United States by investing much of its $43.4 billion bilateral trade surplus in U.S. stocks and bonds. Second, the United States offers much higher interest rates than Japan, typically three to four percentage points higher. Currency losses on paper are not as important to Japanese investors, notably insurance companies, as they often hold bonds until maturity. Nevertheless, Salomon Brothers estimates that Japan's life insurance and casualty companies lost about $3 billion on their $28 billion portfolio of foreign, primarily U.S., securities.[19]   Overall, the Japanese have lost about $15 billion.   To mitigate these heavy currency losses, the Ministry of Finance allows a liberal interpretation of accounting standards.   According to Fortune,

> Japanese financial institutions can carry the bonds at cost without disclosing any exchange losses, as long as losses do not exceed 15 percent in a fiscal year.
> To avoid disclosure, the financial institutions appear to have done fast footwork, loading up on U.S. bonds toward the end of their last fiscal year.   By averaging the relatively modest exchange losses of recently acquired bonds with those bought earlier, the institutions have kept under the 15 percent limit.[20]

While the high savings rate in Japan has been propitious for the United States during its current shortage of domestic capital, the reliance of the U.S. Treasury on a single source of financing is not without risk.   Last May, Japanese investors created a panic in U.S. bond markets when they declined to purchase an offering of Treasury securities.   The Japanese ultimately bought more than half the $9 billion tender but at a yield 400 basis points higher than was originally proffered.   "All this makes two things clear.

---

[19]Edward Boyer, "Foreign Investors Still Love the U.S.," Fortune, May 16, 1986, p. 94.

[20]ibid. p. 96.

First, the Treasury probably won't be able to sell many bonds to the Japanese without a three-point spread. Second, the U.S. Federal Reserve Board probably won't be able to cut interest rates unless the Japanese reduce their domestic rates first."[21]

Although private issues of bonds surpassed Treasury issues in the United States in 1985, Japan has not shown the same interest in private U.S. securities that it has shown in U.S. Treasury securities. With their long-term outlook, the Japanese may feel that the absence of risk offered by the U.S. Government compensates for the lower return.[22] Only since the first quarter of 1986 have net Japanese purchases of U.S. corporate bonds, at $1.9 billion, exceeded their net purchases of U.S. Treasury securities.

Japan purchased only $5.4 billion of private U.S. bonds and $0.3 billion of stocks in 1985. In total, foreigners purchased $4.7 billion of U.S. stocks and $46.0 billion of private U.S. bonds in 1985. Table 9 shows the growth in

---

[21] Edwin A. Finn Jr., "Who's in Charge," Forbes, June 2, 1986, p. 37.

[22] The only risk posed by holding dollar-denominated U.S. Treasury debt is that of U.S. inflation causing a depreciation of the dollar relative to the yen, but the Japanese until recently have not allowed their currency to respond to changes in purchasing power between the United States and Japan.

each of these categories versus U.S. purchases of foreign securities.

TABLE 9

U.S. International Securities Transactions
(billions of dollars, numbers may not total due to rounding)

	U.S. Purchases of Foreign Securities, Public & Private			Foreign Purchases of Private U.S. Securities		
	Total	Stocks	Bonds	Total	Stocks	Bonds
1985	7.9	4.0	3.9	50.7	4.7	46.0
1984	5.1	1.1	3.9	13.0	−0.8	13.8
1983	7.0	3.9	3.1	8.6	6.4	2.2
1982	8.1	1.5	6.6	6.4	3.6	2.8
1981	5.7	0.3	5.4	7.2	5.1	2.1
1980	3.5	2.3	1.2	5.5	4.2	1.2
1979	4.7	0.9	3.8	1.4	1.1	0.3
1978	3.6	−0.5	4.1	2.3	1.3	0.9

Source: U.S. Commerce Department, Survey of Current Business.

If foreigners were investing in the United States because it had the most vital economy and the best hopes for the near future, one would expect to see more investment in U.S. corporate stocks than in bonds. While bonds have fixed payment schedules, stock dividends are more tied to performance. Concern for the health of U.S. industry because of the continuing trade deficits may have made foreigners reluctant to purchase U.S. stocks. If this is the reason for foreign reticence to invest in U.S. stocks, it shows that the Reagan administration's Panglossian faith in the U.S. economy has not always been shared abroad.

Interest Payments and the Current Account

Even as our trade picture improves, the continued rise
in foreign holdings of public and private U.S. bonds will
cause growing interest payments to foreigners and therefore
a steady erosion of the current account balance. By the end
of March 1986, foreigners held $220 billion or 15.1 percent
of the total privately held U.S. Federal debt, receiving
$5.7 billion of interest in that quarter alone. Overall,
foreigners purchased $70.7 billion of U.S. bonds in 1985 and
an estimated $80 billion in 1986. Interest on those bonds
could equal an additional $7 billion annually, on top of the
$57 billion (including bank interest) paid overseas in 1985
by U.S. issuers. Table 10 shows how interest payments have
increased since 1978.

TABLE 10

U.S. Interest Payments to Foreigners, Gross and Net
[Billions of dollars; outflow (-)]

	U.S. Government		Private	
	Gross	Net	Gross	Net
1986 (QI)	(-5.7)	(-4.1)	(-9.6)	(2.3)
1985	-21.3	-15.8	-35.4	14.8
1984	-19.8	-14.6	-38.5	20.8
1983	-17.8	-13.0	-29.2	22.7
1982	-18.3	-14.2	-33.8	24.3
1981	-16.9	-13.2	-28.6	21.6
1980	-12.6	-10.0	-20.9	11.9
1979	-11.1	-8.8	-15.5	8.2
1978	-8.7	-6.9	-8.8	5.1

Source: Survey of Current Business, U.S. Commerce
Department.

Just as the private sector generates a surplus of
savings in the domestic economy, it also generates a surplus
in its holdings of foreign stocks and bonds and in its bank
claims on foreigners. With the public sector, on the other
hand, U.S. Government interest payments (net of receipts)
added almost $16 billion to the $118 billion U.S. current
account deficit in 1985.

The Dollar as an International Asset

There is an important distinction between the interest
payments that the United States must pay and that of other
debtor countries, namely that the United States is able to
pay in its own currency. The United States enjoys this

privilege because the dollar is the key currency in international finance, trade, liquidity formation, and exchange rate agreements. While in some areas the dollar's influence is waning, it does not yet have any viable replacement.

Under the floating rate system, the dollar is still the de facto key currency against which all other currencies are valued. It is argued that only the dollar truly floats, with intervention occuring when it strays too far. Only 16 of the 149 IMF members are considered to have independently floating currencies. All other IMF-member currencies are either under managed float, adjusted according to a set of indicators and limited in their flexibility under cooperative arrangements (such as the European Monetary System), or pegged to either one currency or a basket of currencies. Currently, 31 countries still peg their currencies to the U.S. dollar, approximately half the 1974 number.

In international liquidity formation, the dollar is still the most frequently held currency by central banks, representing 59.9 percent of central bank foreign currency reserves in 1982, compared with 67.6 percent in 1964. The greatest increase in any one currency has been with the European Currency Unit (ECU), a basket of ten currencies from the European Community. Created in 1979, the ECU represented 14.4 percent of international reserves after only three years.

While the importance of the dollar in pegging exchange rates and as a reserve currency has diminished, it is still the currency of international finance and trade. By one rough estimate, almost half of all trade, including many primary commodities such as petroleum, is conducted in dollars. According to a study by the Group of Thirty, "The share of the dollar is fairly large in the invoicing of exports to the United States. With one exception (Japan), it is fairly small in the invoicing of exports to third countries."[23] (Interestingly, 75 percent of Japan's exports to third countries are priced in dollars, compared with three percent for Germany.)

In international finance, the dollar is the most widely used and readily marketable financial asset, partly because of the size of the U.S. equity market. In international capital markets, dollar-denominated Eurobond issues represented 71.3 percent of total Eurobond issues in 1985, while 61.4 percent of external medium-term bank loans were in dollars. The role of the dollar as an accepted financial asset explains why it can retain its exchange value in the face of $150 billion annual trade deficits: its supply and demand are set in the financial markets rather than in the traded goods sector. That is not to imply that large and

---

[23]Peter B. Kenen, "The Role of the Dollar as an International Currency," Group of Thirty, New York, 1983, p. 10.

continued current account deficits have no effect on the
dollar's value, but rather that their effect will now work
through the financial sector. As investors lose confidence
in the U.S. economy because of these deficits, the dollar's
value will fall.

While currency values determined by financial markets
will inevitably be more volatile, they can also be more
easily manipulated by the governments of the major industrial nations. The 40-50 percent decrease in the dollar's
value against major currencies since the finance ministers
of the Group of Five (G-5) met in September 1985 is based on
the speculators' presumption that the G-5 members have the
ability to control currency values. The skill of the G-5
lies not in their mechanistic ability to adjust exchange
rates by changing the supply of each currency, but rather in
their ability to influence demand by preying upon the
short-term thinking and fears of speculators.

The dollar's value cannot remain low for very long
simply because the Federal Reserve Board must maintain
foreigners' interest in holding U.S. assets. To do this,
the Federal Reserve Board must concern itself with both
interest and exchange rates. U.S. interest rates must
remain up to three percentage points higher than those of
Germany and Japan. Rather than having to raise its rates,
the Federal Reserve would prefer to see Germany and Japan
lower theirs.

This presents a problem for the Federal Reserve Board. It must weigh the alternatives of stimulating domestic economic growth against the likelihood of a decline in foreign purchases of U.S. assets. The unilateral decision to lower the discount rate (at which the Federal Reserve Banks lend to commercial banks) in July of 1986 was prompted by the poor performance of the U.S. economy. If the lower rates discourage foreign portfolio investment in the United States, then, because of the need to encourage further inflows of capital, the discount rate cut will be short-lived.

The concern over the exchange rate relates to the fact that foreigners are assuming the exchange risk. If the dollar depreciates, foreign holders of U.S. assets, not the U.S. borrower, suffer the consequences of reduced returns. This is because the debt is denominated in dollars. A run on the dollar could therefore become self-perpetuating, confirming Chairman Volcker's concern that the dollar should fall in an orderly fashion.

Policy Constraints Under Floating Rates

The advent of floating exchange rates was supposed to allow countries to pursue independent economic policies, but, irrevocably, the opposite has occurred. Governments must now, more than ever, take into account the repercussions of domestic economic policies on their international accounts. French attempts at reflation under Mitterand in the early 1980s were greeted by massive capital outflows, leading to repeated currency devaluations. In contrast, U.S. deficit spending pushed up U.S. interest rates thus increasing the foreign demand for U.S. assets. The resulting dollar appreciation helped cause unprecedented and damaging balance of payments deficits.

Divergent economic policies now will affect domestic economies through exchange rates which are in turn a reflection of the supply and demand for one country's assets over another's. The extent to which an economy can withstand the effects of a strong or weak currency partly will determine the degree of autonomy that economy will enjoy. Of the major industrial nations, the United States is the least dependent on trade (see Table 11). In fact, of all the IMF countries surveyed in 1982, only Brazil and Burma had exports constituting a lower percentage of GDP than the United States. Nevertheless, the prolonged appreciation of the dollar until February 1985 and the resulting trade deficit created major dislocations in the U.S. manufacturing sector. In Japan, the appreciation of the yen has led to the first negative quarterly growth in 11 years.

TABLE 11

Exports of Goods and Services as a Percentage
of GDP for Selected Countries, 1982

Germany	33.7
United Kingdom	26.4
Canada	26.0
Italy	24.1
France	21.7
Japan	16.8
United States	8.7

Source: International Financial Statistics, Supplement on
Output Statistics, 1984, IMF.

The Specious Allure of Capital Controls

Faced with the ability of capital movements to under-
mine domestic economic policies, some have called for a
return to the days of capital controls. But are controls
either feasible of desirable? Past experience seems to
indicate that they do not work. Given the increased muta-
bility of capital stemming from the growing sophistication
of investors and financial instruments, controls are even
less likely to work at present. According to C. P.
Kindleberger, "Foreign exchange control has never been
efficient, even in the Nazi period in the 1930s, when

violations carried the death penalty."[24] It is wishful thinking to assume that the U.S. Government can effectively police capital flows when there have been almost $175 billion in unrecorded net capital inflows since 1978 (as revealed by the sum of the "statistical discrepancy" account in the balance of payments).

The argument for capital controls is even weaker than the case for their effectiveness, for they cure the symptoms while ignoring the disease. According to advocates of controls, capital flows, by changing exchange rates, create threats of internecine trade wars. Controlling capital would therefore moderate exchange rate fluctuations. The implied assumption is that trade is more important than investment, but as has been shown in this paper, the two are intricately linked.

If controls had been applied on inflows of capital into the United States since 1981, the dollar might not have appreciated as much, but the additional exports would have been offset by a sharp decline both in investment in productive capacity and in consumer demand in the United States stemming from the higher interest rates. The lack of investment would have rendered U.S. industries less

---

[24]Charles P. Kindleberger and Peter H. Lindert, International Economics (Illinois: Richard D. Irwin, Inc., 1978), p. 446.

competitive internationally, thus increasing the trade deficit. Thus in the most recent example of the United States, controls would have stifled investment while the laissez-faire policies adopted did not. Between 1982 and 1985, gross private domestic investment in the United States grew by 26 percent, including a 34 percent jump in 1984.

Those who argue for capital controls would hope that the high U.S. interest rates from the denial of U.S. access to foreign capital would force Congress and the Administration finally to cut the pernicious budget deficit. But is it sound policy to compound political failures (the budget deficit) with economic misjudgment (capital controls)?

III
Recommendations Concerning Portfolio Investment

Microeconomic Policy Recommendations

This section will focus on microeconomic changes that should be implemented, leaving the macroeconomic suggestions for later. A major problem for policy-makers is in deciding how to remove some of the volatility from capital flows without depriving the United States of the benefits derived from them. One way would be to remove the institutional bias towards short-term thinking in the United States. We are fortunate, in one way, that the principal foreign investors in the United States have been the Japanese with their generally recognized long-term outlook. Few U.S. institutional investors would have kept funds in a country with a currency that lost one third of its value against that investor's home currency in nine months, with the greatest declines occurring in the space of a few weeks.

The best way to effect change in U.S. investment habits would be to use the tax code to promote long-term profits over short-term gains, fees and commissions.[25] Since

---

[25]For a more complete analysis of this proposal, see:
(Footnote Continued)

investment is becoming more and more the domain of institutional investors, primarily pension funds and insurance
companies, such a tax could be fairly narrow in scope.
Although no tax policy ever works as originally intended,
there does seem to be a need for some adjustment in market
thinking.

As pension funds are also major investors overseas, a
more long-term outlook would also reduce currency volatility. There is clearly a need for such a step. In two
consecutive days, the following opening paragraphs were
found in articles in the Journal of Commerce:

> The U.S. dollar pushed broadly higher on remarks
> attributed to Federal Reserve Board Chairman Paul
> Volcker. [26]

> The U.S. dollar fell broadly on new statements by
> Federal Reserve Board Chairman Paul Volcker that the
> market took as bearish for the dollar. [27]

The institutional myopia is a problem that goes beyond
the scope of this report, but there is a clear link between

(Footnote Continued)
Pat Choate and J.K. Linger, "Business and the Short-Term
Syndrome," Washington Post, June 12, 1986.

[26] "Dollar Rises on Volcker Remarks," Journal of
Commerce, June 5, 1986.

[27] "Volcker Testimony Hits Dollar," Journal of Commerce,
June 6, 1986.

capital flows and this phenomenon. As institutional investors expand their international portfolios, this problem
will become more pronounced.

New Macroeconomic Priorities

The United States must elevate the balance of payments
to one of our highest priorities. If not, the continued
erosion of the U.S. current account will weaken our economic
and political preeminence. We can no longer afford to
ignore the international ramifications of domestic policies.
The U.S. economy takes in over one-half of the exports of
the developing countries, New York is one of two international financial centers, and the U.S. dollar is ubiquitous. Thus the United States is granted an unprecedented
importance in the global economy, carrying with it greater
opportunities and greater responsibilities.

The opportunities stem from our ability to pay our way in
dollars, but this benefit is only short-term and should not,
therefore, be taken for granted. Only the United States is
able to issue foreign debt or pay for many imports such as
oil in dollars, without having to earn foreign exchange,
allowing us to postpone unpopular economic adjustments.
While this may be an advantage, it can lead to
irresponsibility on our part because the costs of overcon-
sumption are not as apparent as they would be under a

foreign exchange shortage. People in Congress and in the
Administration start believing that the adjustments can be
postponed forever. This pernicious sense of complacency has
been one of the distinguishing features of U.S. politics in
the 1980s. We will all pay the price in the future; some in
the manufacturing sector are already paying.

The long-term options for the United States are much
less flexible. We have the option of simply printing
dollars to pay off our debt, but such an approach is obvi-
ously inflationary. The only viable alternative is for the
United States to pay off its debts. As has been shown in
this report, the foreign capital is going mostly into liquid
U.S. bonds rather than into U.S. plant and equipment, and as
a result, we face a declining standard of living in order to
divert precious capital to debt service. The United States
sent $57 billion in gross interest payments to foreigners in
1985.

The fact that the U.S. Treasury can pay interest to
foreigners in dollars grants only a temporary respite from
the inevitable deflation that accompanies overspending. In
addition, if the inflow of foreign capital pushes up the
exchange rate, foreign financing of U.S. public debt can
have a depressing effect on U.S. production. So while the
U.S. Treasury has had to assume no exchange risk on its
foreign debt, as a result of the high dollar, U.S.
industries have been forced to retrench or to source
offshore.

In light of the freedom from exchange risk bestowed upon U.S. borrowers by virtue of the dollar's role, the U.S. Treasury should think twice before promoting the internationalization of the yen simply to cause an appreciation of that currency. As long as U.S. budget deficits persist, any decline in the importance of the dollar will not be in the interest of the U.S. Treasury.

The greater responsibilities the United States must undertake include a cognizance of the effect of our policies on our allies and on the poorer nations. While the maintenance of an open market for goods and services by the Reagan administration in the face of damaging trade deficits is commendable, our insouciance towards global capital flows has been reprehensible. We are swallowing up a significant portion of the world's savings for our own consumption. No developing country can compete with the United States for capital in international financial markets.

U.S. Policies Toward Capital

Typically, U.S. international economic policy has concentrated on trade issues rather than confronting the more abstruse problem of capital flows. Opening up foreign economies to our direct investment has been largely ignored or even hampered. Assuring the ascendancy of New York as the world's financial center also has not been a high priority of policy makers. In fact, the controls on capital in the United States in the 1970s augmented the Euromarket at the expense of New York. It must be recognized that capital flows largely determine trade flows, not the opposite. Direct investment promotes exports while portfolio investment affects trade through the exchange rate. Increased U.S. holdings of foreign financial assets would cause other currencies to appreciate. Therefore, while Congress and the USTR should continue to open up foreign markets to U.S. goods, they must also strive to open markets to foreign investment. Not only would the increased investment spur exports, but the income from that investment would accrue to the current account.

Liberalization of portfolio flows must proceed slowly. If not, events can sometimes occur before countries have developed an adequate policy response. The recent imbalances in net capital flows have caught governments by surprise. There were no well-developed policy mechanisms for dealing with the prolonged appreciation of the dollar in the 1980s. Although such markets as the Euromarket have functioned well without regulation for years, countries should be wary of increasing the volatility of flows.

Macroeconomic Coordination

Apart from the microeconomic changes suggested, governments can reduce the harmful volatility and overshooting of
exchange rates through macroeconomic coordination of
monetary and fiscal policies. Unfortunately, the degree of
coordination envisioned by U.S. Treasury Secretary Baker at
the Tokyo economic summit is probably not feasible at this
point in time. Germany, Japan, and the United States all
have different policy objectives and all have historical
aversions to different economic phenomena such as inflation
in West Germany and unemployment in the United States. The
best that can be hoped for at present, other than coordinated intervention in the currency markets and an occasional synchronized cut in interest rates, is a series of
unilateral actions taken by each of the three countries that
together serve to reduce imbalances. However, U.S. policy
should not be guided by a presumption that our trading
partners will significantly adjust their internal economic
policies for the benefit of others.

Unilateral Actions by Japan and West Germany

Although this report is primarily concerned with the
U.S. response to global economic events, there is an obvious
need for complementary programs initiated by our major

economic allies. The Reagan administration has asked
Germany to use fiscal policy to expand the German economy,
but Germany is not likely to do so because of the example of
the late 1970s when it complied with U.S. requests during
the Carter administration to become the locomotive to spur
the European and the global economy. The result was inflation and more unemployment.

With Japan, U.S. recommendations are much more
far-reaching, following along the lines of a report by a
commission appointed by Japanese Prime Minister Nakasone and
chaired by a former governor of the Bank of Japan, Haruo
Maekawa. The commission essentially calls for a
restructuring of the Japanese economy away from export-led
growth and more towards increasing domestic demand.
Achieving a national consensus in Japan on such a dramatic
change of emphasis is likely to prove difficult. The United
States is correct in pushing Japan in the direction of
taking on a role in the international economy commensurate
with its economic wealth. But we should be careful not to
have Japan reduce its national savings rate before we have
reduced our dependence on Japanese capital and before an
adequate mechanism to supply capital to the Third World in
sufficient quantities has been developed. Furthermore, we
should not delude ourselves into thinking that the Japanese
will be any more forthcoming in achieving the desired
results here than they have been with seven major trade
liberalization schemes in the 1980s.

U.S. Actions

The United States needs its own version of the Maekawa Commission Report. While Congress has looked inappropriately into an industrial policy, the President has appointed various groups to study U.S. industrial competitiveness or international private enterprise. Both Congress and the Administration also have discussed reorganizing the executive branch through a Department of Trade. But all such approaches have been piecemeal.

The United States does not need another department or a new commission. What it needs is greater coordination at the White House level of all of the conflicting economic, political and strategic interests. U.S. international economic policy should not be set by the Defense or State Departments, or by the White House Chief of Staff. The present emphasis on strategic and political interests over our basic international economic rights eventually will impinge on all of our interests by increasing the long-term economic tensions between the United States and its allies. In this regard, the President should appoint an Economic Security Advisor along the lines of the National Security Advisor. The ESA should be of sufficient stature to enable his or her views to prevail over the competing interests of the various Departments. The position of Chairman of the Council of Economic Advisors is of insufficient stature to perform this role.

At the very least, the public debate over international economic issues should be expanded so as to increase the general awareness of the U.S. and global economic nexus. Some significant legislation has been passed with little thought to its global economic consequences. For example, the breakup of AT&T opened up a whole new market worth billions of dollars to foreign companies with nothing in return. In the area of tax reform, other than its effect on domestic capital formation, very little attention was given to the international effects of proposed legislation.

America no longer has an economic surplus with which to bestow favorable trade or economic benefits on others. When access to foreign markets is impeded, we must push for openness. Like in military strategy, America should steer away from a first strike, but must be willing to react to other barriers in the second instance. This means taking action to mandate fair, open and reciprocal treatment. Both trade and investment must be considered part of the same economic pie and must be guided by the same principles.

In addition to overall policy recommendations, there are a number of tangible suggestions that are all related to the theme of improving our national rate of savings. Without such a step, we face a prolonged dependence on foreign capital and/or structurally high interest rates.

The national savings is expressed by the following equation:

$(S-I) + (T-G)$ = the current account balance;

where S: gross private savings

I: gross private domestic investment

T: Government (Federal and State) revenues

G: Government spending

When there is not enough domestic savings to fund expenditures and investments, the shortfall is covered by inflows of capital. Thus, the current account balance is roughly equal to U.S. inflows of foreign capital. Table 11 shows the relationship between private and public savings and the current account.

TABLE 12

Savings, Investment, and the Current Account
(billions of dollars)

	Net Private Savings (S-I)	Net Public Savings (T-G)	Net National Savings (S-I)+(T-G)	Current Account
1985	26	−140	−114	−118
1984	19	−109	−90	−107
1983	100	−135	−35	−46
1982	109	−115	−6	−8
1981	26	−27	−1	6
1980	33	−31	2	2
	313	−557	−244	−271

Considering the size of the numbers involved, it can be seen that the equation has held fairly well for the last six years, yielding a discrepancy of only $41 billion. Significantly, the private sector has paid its own way: since 1980, gross private savings (S) have exceeded gross private domestic investment (I) by $313.6 billion. Gross private savings are comprised mainly of personal savings, undistributed corporate profits, and capital consumption allowances.

If the private sector invested more than it saved, inflows of foreign capital presumably would be invested in productive capacity. With the dissavings in the public sector, the inflow has gone to current consumption by the Federal government. While the Federal deficit was exacerbated by the tax cuts under the Economic Recovery and Tax Act (ERTA) of 1981, state and local governments managed a surplus of $58.7 billion in 1985. The greatest increase in the deficit since 1980 has come mostly from increased expenditures, particularly defense spending (89 percent for defense and 52 percent for nondefense).

The current account deficit (equal to capital inflows plus a sizable statistical discrepancy) is a reflection of the imbalance between net private and public savings. To improve the current account balance, we need to reduce our dependence on foreign capital, either by increasing net private savings or by decreasing net public dissavings. The private sector can be influenced most directly through the tax code and it is for this reason that the tax reform passed by Congress in 1986 should have been analyzed very carefully for its effects on private savings and investment.

On the savings side, the tax reform could be disastrous. The Act lengthens depreciation schedules and increases corporate taxes enormously, thus cutting corporate savings. Personal savings are reduced by the elimination of the individual retirement accounts (IRAs). It is possible that the nondeductibility of many kinds of interest expense will promote savings over borrowing among individuals, but this effect is unlikely to offset the drop in corporate savings. Yet, corporate savings, unlike Government spending, fuel economic growth through long-term investment rather than current consumption.

In terms of private investment, the tax reform will cut into corporate investment through radical surgery on the investment tax credit, harming those heavy manufacturing industries most affected by the high dollar, such as steel and automobiles. However, the area of services or those businesses whose assets are "people" will benefit from the reform.

These issues clearly transcend the popular notions that corporations do not pay their fair share of taxes. International competition should not be used to justify a completely laissez-faire attitude towards business, but when rewriting the tax code, legislators should look at the effects of tax reform on our current account and at the taxation of corporations in other countries. It is this kind of thinking in a vacuum that does the most damage to our economy.

If the U.S. Government wants to reduce the trade deficit and the magnitude of capital inflows and thus reduce the threat posed by volatility, the best way would be to reduce the savings deficit of the Federal government. As can be seen by the savings equation, the Government could either decrease expenditures, raise taxes, or do some combination of both. Politics will decide which variable to alter and by how much. If the savings deficit is not reduced, then the normal course of economic cycles will make the adjustment for us through a recession and reduced consumption.

Conclusion

There are essentially two issues central to the discussion of capital flows into the United States. The first, caused by the U.S. economy's inability to generate enough private savings to offset the Federal deficit, is the growing reliance of the U.S. economy on foreign capital. The U.S. Government must be held accountable, both for this deficit and for the relatively low rate of savings in the private sector. Without steps to remedy these two shortcomings, U.S. debt to foreigners will increase, and we risk losing our special status as the only country that can pay its foreign debt in its own currency. The United States then would be forced to curtail its extensive presence overseas, as the British did in the 1960s when it pulled back from its "East of Suez" commitments.

In addition to our potentially impoverished international posture, the United States also faces constraints at home. Interest rates must remain several percentage points higher than those in Japan and West Germany, and inflation must be kept at bay to retain confidence in U.S. assets. Domestic policy will be guided by international forces.

The second issue concerns the volatility of capital flows. Billions of dollars can be sent out of a country before it has the chance to respond. To reduce this volatility, the Government should work to remove the imbalances that spur capital flows. A stable and coordinated international economic environment would reduce some of the most egregious speculation and thus serve to stabilize exchange rates.

About the Authors

Ronald L. Danielian is president and a director of the International Economic Policy Association. In his career with that Association, he has served as its executive vice president and treasurer and director of its Center for Multinational Studies from 1974 to 1984. Mr. Danielian was formerly director, Office of Research and Analysis, United States Travel Service, U.S. Department of Commerce, where he was responsible for balance of payments and market research studies, and represented the agency before Congressional committees, the OECD, and other international bodies. Prior to 1971 he was the Assistant and Associate Economist at IEPA and has worked in senatorial offices on Capitol Hill.

Mr. Danielian has completed more than a dozen economic surveys of Europe, Latin America, and the Far East. He has written a number of IEPA Confidential Reporters and other analyses of international economic issues including trade, investment, taxation, raw materials and international service industry questions.

After graduation from Aurora University (Illinois), Mr. Danielian studied at American University. He is the author of Services in America's International Trade: The Air Travel and Tourism Sector, 1978, and The United States Flag System in International Air Commerce: An Analysis of Public Policy Implications, 1974.

He is a co-author of: U.S. Foreign Economic Strategy for the Eighties, 1982, and The United States Balance of Payments: A Reappraisal, 1968. He has served as a consultant to the U.S. Department of Commerce, and is a founder, vice president, and a trustee of the International Economic Studies Institute where he was a contributing author to the book, Raw Materials & Foreign Policy, 1976.

Stephen E. Thomsen was an economist on the Association's staff for three years. He majored in economics at Middlebury College where he received the Bachelor of Arts degree, studied economics at L'Institute d'Etudes Politiques and L'Universite de Paris-X, and received the Master of International Management degree from the American Graduate School of International Management. He is currently a doctoral candidate at the Graduate Institute of International Studies in Geneva, Switzerland.

Mr. Thomsen is the author of International Capital Flows and the United States: Palliative, Panacea or Pandora's Box, 1985. He has contributed to a number of the Association's studies and its Issues and Answers series. While he was at the International Economic Policy Association, he supervised its research program.

Index